POETICA

SEHAJPREET KAUR

Copyright © Sehajpreet Kaur
All Rights Reserved.

This book has been published with all efforts taken to make the material error-free after the consent of the author. However, the author and the publisher do not assume and hereby disclaim any liability to any party for any loss, damage, or disruption caused by errors or omissions, whether such errors or omissions result from negligence, accident, or any other cause.

While every effort has been made to avoid any mistake or omission, this publication is being sold on the condition and understanding that neither the author nor the publishers or printers would be liable in any manner to any person by reason of any mistake or omission in this publication or for any action taken or omitted to be taken or advice rendered or accepted on the basis of this work. For any defect in printing or binding the publishers will be liable only to replace the defective copy by another copy of this work then available.

To my dreams which lead me so far.

Contents

Contents

Preface

Not really focusing on a particular theme, I wanted to let my mind go free, I wanted to let it wander, and hence here I end up with a compilation of poems on all sorts of random themes. Being a person who cannot focus on one thing at a time, I did face a bit of difficulty while I penned these down and it took pretty long too.

I ought to improve as I write more of these in the future.

Acknowledgements

I won't be very specific, but to be honest all those who are reading this, know that I would thank all of you, for reading this book of mine, for acknowledging me. Thank you.

1. The Blue Butterfly

Still stuck at the time,
When it came by,
And brushed by my cheek,
A Blue Butterfly.

2. The Lake

That lake of water,
It looked so calm,
I wish it taught me,
To stay away from harm.

3. A White Swan

A white swan,
As it flutters it's wings,
Down the river,
Along the water it swings.
It's as white as snow,
With a heart so pure,
Down the river it goes,
Looking for more.

4. The Nightmare Witch

In my nightmare,
I saw a witch,
Mom said who talks too much,
She puts a stitch.
Since the night,
I've been quiet and behaved,
Afraid she'll come,
And I'll be slaved.

5. Which Colour ?

White for good,
Black for bad,
Bright for happy ,
And dark for sad.
But I'd rather say,
It's us humans who did,
The division of these,
Else, all colours are beautiful indeed.

6. A Flower

It was soft and pink,
Right close to my hand,
As it touched my skin,
Startled I stand.
Then putting my face close,
I focused on it,
A tender flower,
A true beauty, I must admit.

7. Flawless ?

I must look fair,
As slim as anyone could see,
Round eyes and rosy cheeks,
A flawless woman I want to be.
What is flawless?
In the world's eyes,
It's just torture,
To end your true self, it would suffice.
Love yourself,
You are pretty enough,
Your confident walk,
Makes you strong and tough.

8. Lost In A Book

Flipping through the pages,
It was deeper each time,
Trying to know what will happen,
In the very next line.
Is this how you feel,
When you are lost in a book,
You fall in love with it,
With just a mere look.

9. The Circle Of Life

To work hard and run ahead,
Is what we're taught since we're five,
Well, this is how it works,
The circle of life.
It'll teach you to compete,
To be your best self,
In order to succeed,
To be the top on the shelf.

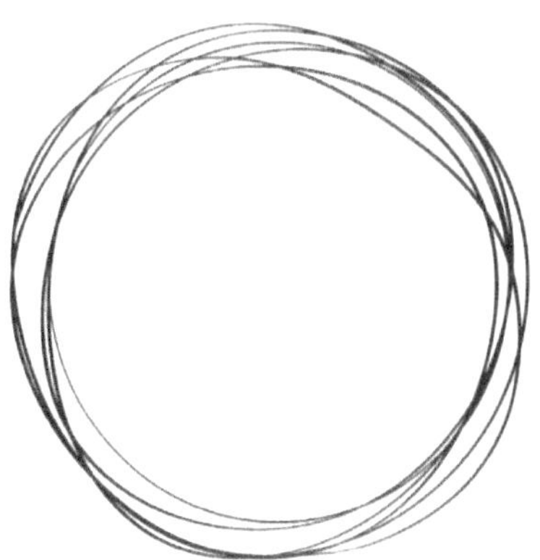

10. Coffee ?

Half a cup of water,

In a pan,

Put it on the flame,

Add in a spoon of sugar as the boiling began.

As it dissolves,

Quarter a teaspoon of coffee powder,

To have the perfect aroma,

Just as fragrant as a flower.

Then put half a cup milk,

Here it goes in the pan,

Let it all boil,

Then pour in a mug,

The perfect plan!

11. A Raindrop

It fell on me,
So sudden yet soft,
Felt it with my hand,
It was a raindrop.
Crystal clear,
And yet so pure,
So calm yet pleasing,
Like the heaven's door.

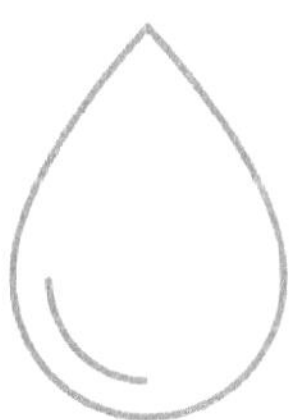

12. A True Promise

A true promise is what's done,
With love and trust,
And kept for years to come.

13. A Tale Of Colors

The sweet pink,
The berry blue,
The creamy white,
A deep clue.
The dark black,
The smart yellow,
The decent red,
A fresh fellow.
The story of colors,
Too deep to interpret,
Just look at 'em all,
You don't want to regret.

14. A Forest Dream

I look around,
The forest so green,
And then I wake up,
From the sweetest dream.

15. My Favourite Color

My favourite colour ?
It tastes like love,
It tastes like summer,
It tastes like trust.
It tastes like friendship,
It tastes so sweet,
It tastes like comfort,
It tastes so complete.
Try to guess what it is,
It might be easy,
But tough as it is,
'Cos my favourite colour's a total treat.

16. My Love

She put it on my lap,
Her wet round snout,
Just as moving she could look,
Her whines are so loud.
As white as snow,
With a brown spot round the eye,
A slim little waist,
And not at all shy.
She would bark all the time,
If you tease her with a treat,
Might even snatch it out your hand,
Then would rush to a corner to eat.
A thin long tail,
With a pointy end,
She's our little love,
An angel god had sent.

(Dedicated to my 1 year old dog, who's still with me and will be for years to come. I love you Ziggy.)

17. Expectations

Expectations,
Are weapons of hell.
They can make your mind sound and well,
And can crush you enough to feel unwell.

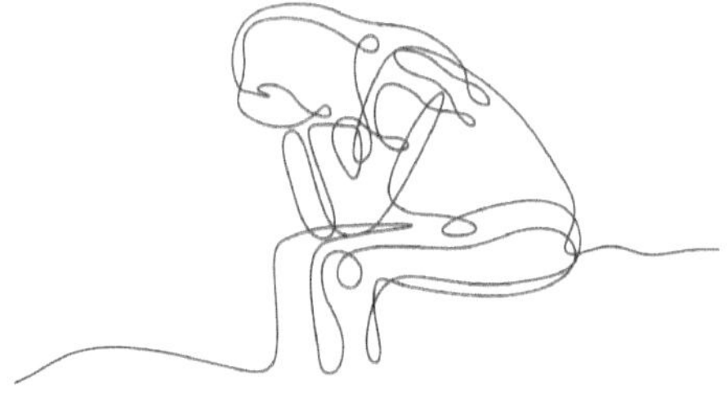

18. The Bright Side

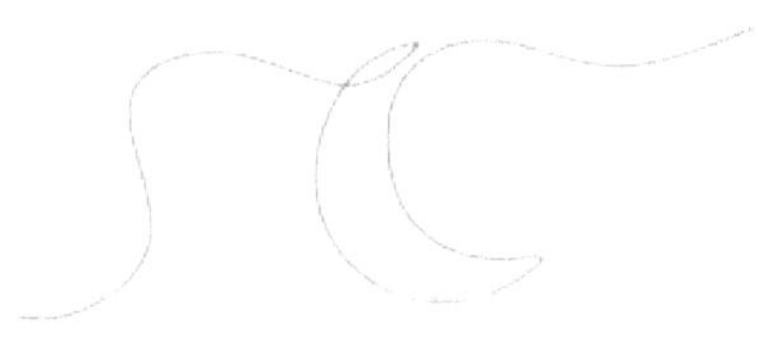

19. An Uncertain Dream

Jumping with joy,
Towards that uncertain dream,
Waited for this so long,
To the vending machine.
Going near it,
I face it with a smile,
'Out of order' it said,
Running out of hope, a gloomy little child.

20. The Treat Of Life

Down the lane,
The baker's shop,
Sweet cakes,
With sour cream on top.
Gives us a taste of life,
With sweet times,
Come moments too,
Moments so, as sour as lime.

21. The Hardest Goodbye

It was the hardest goodbye,
Seeing him go away,
Wrapped in those particles of soil,
Covered with those pearls of salt.
Tear-filled eyes,
Not knowing what to do,
He lay there so still,
'Daniel' I'll miss you.

(To my precious little puppy, Daniel, whom we lost on 11.07.2020. You will forever be missed Daniel.)

22. The Balloon Seller

He came shouting,
In a funny disguise,
I ran to him,
With sparkles in my eyes.
Two for me,
I said as I reached,
With a smile on his face he handed me,
Two balloons that he unleashed.

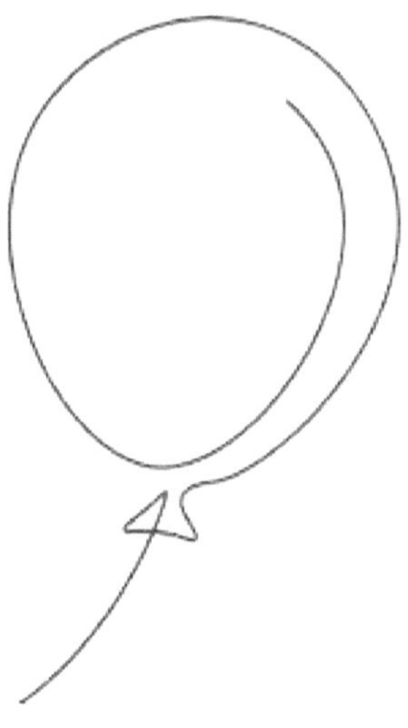

23. Does It Hurt ?

It is sad,
When it hurts you so bad,
When you can't even stand,
When there seems to be no end.

24. Fire

A flame of fire,
With souls of the liars,
With unfulfilled desires.
Bright yellow it burns,
With flames rising high,
Ambitions so hot,
Reaching the sky.

25. A Feminine Colour

Red and white,
To form pink,
A color, very feminine.

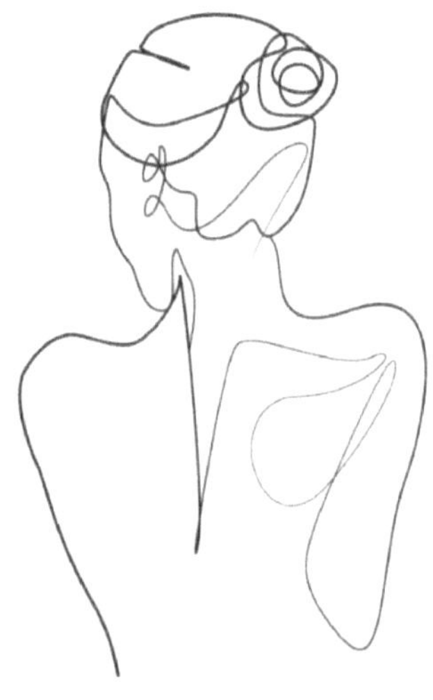

26. Does It ?

A mountain turned upside down,
A cloud on top should be seen,
Does it look familiar?
Does it look like an ice cream?

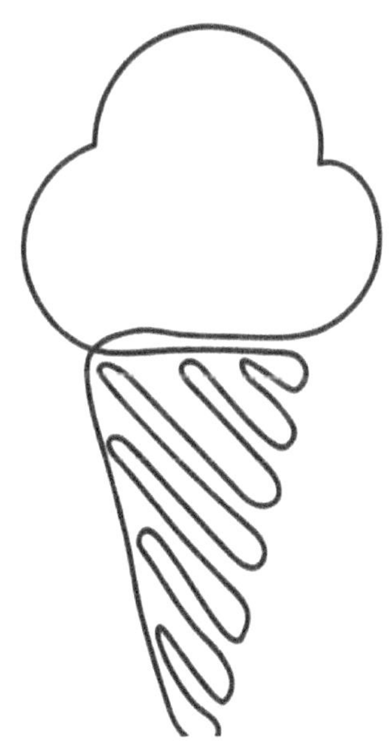

27. Music

Music is a wave,
It is a feeling,
It may make you cry so easily,
Yet be so healing.
It runs through your body,
Makes you feel at ease,
It relates with your story,
With your decision it agrees.

28. The Sunset

I know its time,
When the light is scattered,
With a beautiful orange blanket,
When the sky is covered.

The environment is calm,
And a cool breeze blows,
The sky gets darker,
And down the sun goes.

29. The First Meal I Cooked

The first meal I cooked,
Was a total disaster,
Salt a little too much,
The chilli was the queen hereafter.
A bit too watery,
And the texture so bland,
The ingredients were raw,
Well, it was my first time, you should understand.

30. Cotton Candy

So soft and colourful,
So tempting to eat,
It feels like cotton ,
Yet tastes so sweet.

31. Tea

Hot and relieving,
With a rising steam,
Sip it up a bit,
A cup of warm tea.

Author's Diary

A very normal girl who 'kind of' fell in love with poetry at the age of 12.

I did not really read poetry but rather wrote more. I still remember going to a friend's birthday party and she was handing us signs with nicknames she kept for each one of us. And mine said 'Poet'.

But I do sometimes think that I am not that good and that ofcourse others can and will do way better than me. Despite that I know that there is something in me that is still driving me, putting my heart's choice above anything. And I really appreciate that 'Something' in me. It is what inspired me to complete this small poetry compilation of poems that I wrote. Even though I know some people might not even like it, they might not even bother, still, something in me tells me, " Atlest the rest of the 'Few' will like it."

That is what drives me.

Today I am 15, when I wrote this book. It took me 3 years to gather that confidence that yes my poems were worth reading.

I really appreciate and thank my younger self for trusting herself.

Incase You Are Reading This ?

If you read this far, I really appreciate and thank you for being so important to me. Staying and reading my book till the very end is really really really a very special feeling for me. Thank You.

www.ingramcontent.com/pod-product-compliance
Lightning Source LLC
Chambersburg PA
CBHW031247130726
47988CB00008B/3274